C000001296

THE WISDOM
OF
SAINT COLUMBA
OF IONA

The Wisdom
Of
Saint Columba
Of Iona

Compiled and introduced by Murray Watts

Published by
Lion Publishing plc
Sandy Lane West, Oxford, England
ISBN 0 7459 3841 8

First edition 1997
10 9 8 7 6 5 4 3 2 1

A catalogue record for this book is
available from the British Library

Printed and bound in Singapore

Series editor: Philip Law

Commissioning editor: Meryl Doney

Project editor: Angela Handley

Book designer: Nicholas Rous

Jacket designer: Gerald Rogers

Text Acknowledgments

*Celtic Christian Spirituality: An Anthology of
Medieval and Modern Sources*, O. Davies and
F. Bowie, 1995: pages 10, 34. Used by
permission of SPCK. *Iona, the Earliest
Poetry of a Celtic Monastery*, trans. by
T.O. Clancy and G. Markus, 1995:
pages 11, 18, 27, 28, 32, 33, 35, 36, 39.
Used by permission of Edinburgh
University Press. *Celtic Fire* by Robert van
de Weyer, published and copyright 1990,
by Darton, Longman and Todd Ltd (UK)
and Bantam, Doubleday Dell Publishing
Group Inc. (US): page 12. Used by
permission of the publishers. *Carmina
Gadelica*, Alexander Carmichael, 1928:
pages 13, 14, 24, 30, 46. Used by
permission of Scottish Academic Press.
Manus O'Donnell, 1532, quoted in
Celtic Christianity: Ecology and Holiness
by C. Bamford and W.P. Marsh, 1986,
used by permission of Lindisfarne Books,
Hudson N.Y.: page 23. *Life of St Columba*,
Richard Sharpe, 1995: page 41.

Picture Acknowledgments

The cover illustration is reproduced from
the *Book of Kells* with the permission of
The Board of Trinity College, Dublin.
Detail is reproduced by permission of the
Bodleian Library, Oxford (MS. Gough
Liturg. 2, fol. 82r). All illustrations in
the text are reproduced from *The Book of
Kells*, (folios 2r, 5r, 19v, 27v, 32v, and
34r) with the permission of The Board
of Trinity College, Dublin.

CONTENTS

Introduction

In the first few minutes of Whit Sunday, on 9 June 597, a monk died on a tiny island off the west coast of Scotland. He lay on the altar steps of the oratory, his face radiant with joy. It was the end of a pilgrimage which is still remembered and celebrated throughout the celtic world 1400 years later.

Columba was born in 521, in Gartan Donegal, a prince of the Cinell Connall Clan. He might well have become the High King of Ireland, had he not forsaken everything for the sake of the 'High King of Heaven'. His Irish name, Columcille, means 'the dove of the church', and he was to found many churches. His character is associated with miraculous powers, prophetic wisdom, the crowning of kings and the spread of Christianity throughout Ireland and Scotland. He can justly be called one of the founding fathers of the Scottish nation and, in many ways, its true patron saint.

No monk, in the history of these islands, has ever commanded such overwhelming respect from kings and clerics, rich and poor. He was greatly loved and, by some, greatly feared. For in Columba, everyone who met him sensed the presence of God.

But, according to tradition, 'the dove of the church' began life with another, unflattering, name: Crimthan, the fox, and some of his earlier years can be seen as a story of tribal intrigue. The historical facts are shrouded in legend, but it seems clear that he became involved in a terrible battle at Cul Drevny in 561. Columba's clan and his allies were victorious but 3000 of the enemy were slain. According to the poets and writers of later centuries, this was why he left Ireland for ever, in an act of supreme penance. He sailed to the island of Iona and founded a monastery.

Columba is a profoundly sympathetic figure, a man of failures and struggles, but much of what he fought for in his own life can only be described as deeply unfashionable today. His quest was anything but comfortable. 'Spiritual tourists', hoping to pick up a few souvenirs from the kingdom of God – candles in the shape of celtic crosses, postcards of the Book of Kells – while ignoring their own souls, would be well-advised to avoid any encounter with St Columba. Yet, precisely because he is an uncomfortable character as well as being so deeply attractive, we should listen to him. Columba's voice was once renowned for its rare beauty and power, and he is still singing to us down the centuries.

Columba is the archetype of the 'peregrinatus', the wanderer or pilgrim who abandons security for a journey which is extremely costly, and yet whose reward is ultimately everlasting life. His physical journey was not a matter of many miles, but his spiritual journey measured a vast distance from worldly influence to the role of a servant of others. The celtic christians had a name for this kind of journey: it was called 'white martyrdom'. This undramatic christian sacrifice involves many daily deaths and simple denials but produces a character transfigured by the presence of love. It is a journey which celebrates the immense richness of creation and gradually brings the joyful awareness of the power of God in every area of life.

Perhaps no words can express the wisdom of Columba as eloquently, and with such compelling simplicity, as the earliest tribute to him, from around 600, the *Amra Choluimb Chille*: 'He was the perfect sage, he believed Christ.'

MURRAY WATTS

Freswick, Caithness

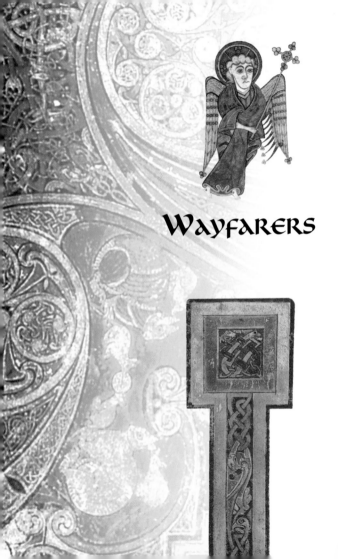

Wayfarers

THE PATH

The path I walk, Christ walks it.
May the land in which I am be without sorrow.
May the Trinity protect me wherever I stay,
Father, Son and Holy Spirit.
Bright angels walk with me – dear presence –
in every dealing.

May I arrive at every place, may I return home;
may the way in which I spend be without loss.
May every path before me be smooth,
man, woman and child welcome me.
A truly good journey!
Well does the fair Lord show us a course, a path.

'The Protection of Columcille', attributed to Columba

THE PRIZE

He left Ireland, entered a pact,
he crossed in ships the whales' shrine.
He shattered lusts – it shone on him –
a bold man over the sea's ridge.

He fought wise battles with the flesh,
indeed, he read pure learning.
He stitched, he hoisted sail tops,
a sage across seas, his prize a kingdom.

Beccán mac Luigdech, poet and hermit from Iona

THE QUESTIONS

Shall I abandon, O King of Mysteries, the soft comforts of home? Shall I turn my back on my native land, and my face towards the sea?

Shall I put myself wholly at the mercy of God, without silver, without a horse, without fame and honour?

Shall I say farewell to my beautiful land, placing myself under Christ's yoke? Shall I pour out my heart to him, confessing my manifold sins and begging forgiveness, tears streaming down my cheeks?

Shall I leave the prints of my knees on the sandy beach, a record of my final prayer in my native land? Shall I then suffer every kind of wound that the sea can inflict?

Shall I take my tiny coracle across the wide, sparkling ocean? O King of the Glorious Heaven, shall I go of my own choice upon the sea?

O Christ, will you help me on the wild waves?

Attributed to St Brendan, contemporary of Columba

THE GOSPEL OF THE GOD OF LIFE

The Gospel of the God of life
  To shelter thee, to aid thee;
Yea, the Gospel of beloved Christ
  The holy Gospel of the Lord;

To keep thee from all malice,
  From every dole and dolour;
To keep thee from all spite,
  From evil eye and anguish.

Thou shalt travel thither, thou shalt travel hither,
  Thou shalt travel hill and headland,
Thou shalt travel down, thou shalt travel up,
  Thou shalt travel ocean and narrow.

Christ Himself is shepherd over thee,
  Enfolding thee on every side;
He will not forsake thee hand or foot,
  Nor let evil come anigh thee.

Carmina Gadelica

GUIDANCE

O Thou who pervadest the heights,
Imprint on us Thy gracious blessing,
Carry us over the surface of the sea,
Carry us safely to a haven of peace…

I myself will sit down at the helm,
It is God's own Son who will give me guidance,
As He gave to Columba the mild
What time he set stay to sails.

Carmina Gadelica

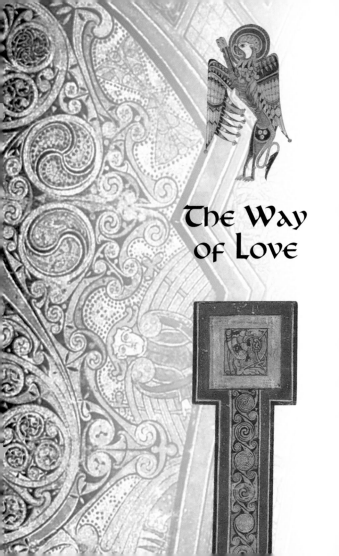

The Way
of Love

CONTEMPLATION

Delightful would it be to me to be in Uchd Ailiun
    On the pinnacle of a rock,
That I might often see
    The face of the ocean;
That I might see its heaving waves
    Over the wide ocean,
When they chant music to their Father
    Upon the world's course;
That I might see its level sparkling strand,
    It would be no cause of sorrow;
That I might hear the song of the wonderful birds,
    Source of happiness;
That I might hear the thunder of the crowding
        waves
    Upon the rocks;
That I might hear the roar by the side of the
        church
    Of the surrounding sea;
That I might see its noble flocks
    Over the watery ocean;

That I might see the sea monsters,
  The greatest of all wonders;
That I might see its ebb and flood
  In their career;
That my mystical name might be, I say,
  Cul ri Erin;*
That contrition might come upon my heart
  Upon looking at her;
That I might bewail my evils all,
  Though it were difficult to compute them;
That I might bless the Lord
  Who conserves all,
Heaven with its countless bright orders,
  Land, strand and flood;
That I might search the books all,
  That would be good for my soul;
At times kneeling to beloved Heaven;
  At times psalm singing;
At times contemplating the King of Heaven.

Attributed to Columba

* '*Back turned to Ireland*'.

LIGHT IN THE DARKNESS

As a lantern raises its light in a dark house, so truth rises in the midst of faith in a person's heart. Four darknesses it expels when it rises there: the darkness of paganism, the darkness of ignorance, the darkness of doubt, the darkness of sin, so that none of them can find room there.

The Alphabet of Devotion

TRUE WORSHIP

O Living God!
Alas for him who evil works!
That which he thinks not of, comes to him;
That which he hopes, vanishes out of his hand.
There is no magic that can tell our fate,
Nor bird upon the branch,
Nor trunk of gnarled oak…

Better is He in whom we trust,
The King who has made us all,
Who will not leave me tonight without refuge.
I adore not the voice of birds
Nor chance, nor the love of a son or a wife,
My druid is Christ, the Son of God,
The Son of Mary, the Great Abbot,
The Father, the Son and the Holy Spirit.

From The Song of Trust, attributed to Columba

THE LABOUR OF LOVING

The love of God with all thy heart and all thy
  strength.
The love of thy neighbour as thyself.
Abide in the Testaments of God throughout all
  times.
Thy measure of prayer shall be until thy tears
  come;
Or thy measure of work of labour till thy tears
  come;
Or thy measure of thy work of labour, or of
  thy genuflexions, until thy perspiration
  often comes, if thy tears are not free.

From the Rule of St Columba

WELCOME ONE ANOTHER

Forget thy poverty awhile;
Let us think of the world's hospitality.
The Son of Mary will prosper thee
And every guest shall have his share.
Many a time
What is spent returns to the bounteous hand,
And that which is kept back
None the less has passed away.

From The Song of Trust

RUNE OF HOSPITALITY

I saw a stranger yestreen:
I put food in the eating place,
Drink in the drinking place,
Music in the listening place:

And in the sacred name of the Triune
He blessed myself and my house,
My cattle and my dear ones.
And the lark said in her song
    Often, often, often
Goes the Christ in the stranger's guise,
    Often, often, often
Goes the Christ in the stranger's guise.

Traditional Gaelic

IONA

Behold Iona!
A blessing on each eye that seeth it!
He who does a good for others
Here, will find his own redoubled
    Many-fold!

Attributed to Columba

THE CALL TO PEACE

Peace between neighbours,
Peace between kindred,
Peace between lovers,
    In love of the King of life.

Peace between person and person,
Peace between wife and husband,
Peace between woman and children,
    The peace of Christ above all peace.

Carmina Gadelica

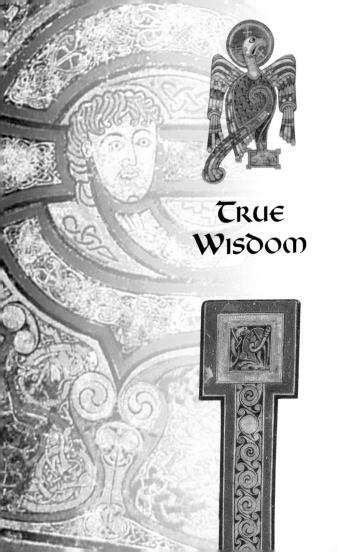

True Wisdom

THE SERVANT

There was not born of the Gaidhel, however, a being more illustrious, or more wise, or of better family, than Columcille. There came not of them any person who was more modest, more humble, or more lowly.

Great indeed was the humility of Columcille, for it was he himself that used to take their shoes off his monks, and that used to wash their feet for them. 'Tis he that used often to take his share of corn on his back to the mill, and that used to grind it and bring it home with him. 'Tis he that would not have linen or wool to his skin, that would not sleep until his side came in contact with the bare earth. Under his head there used not to be but a pillar-stone for a pillow...

From the old Irish Life of St Columba

THE CHRISTIAN LIFE

What is best for the Christian life? Simplicity and single-mindedness. A careless Christianity which resists great bother, its trial in fire will be great, its reward in Heaven will be small. An active Christianity which resists great comfort, its trial in fire will be small, its reward in Heaven will be great.

What is best for the mind? Breadth and humility, for every good thing finds room in a broad, humble mind. What is worst for the mind? Narrowness and closedness, and constrictedness, for nothing good finds room in a narrow, closed, restricted mind.

The Alphabet of Devotion

WISDOM AND JUSTICE

He is not truly wise who is
not just. For true wisdom
cannot find room with
injustice in a person, for the
veil is thick between them.
For his justice is nearer to
meeting with wisdom than is
his wisdom with justice, for
it is then that a person is
truly wise, when he is just.

The Alphabet of Devotion

IDLE WORDS

A person too who would talk
with thee in idle words, or of
the world; or who murmurs
at what he cannot remedy or
prevent, but who would
distress thee more should he
be a tattler between friends
and foes, thou shalt not
admit him to thee, but
at once give him thy
benediction should he
deserve it.

From the Rule of St Columba

INVOCATION

The tongue of Columba in my head,
The eloquence of Columba in my speech;
The composure of the Victorious Son of grace
    Be mine in presence of the multitude.

Carmina Gadelica

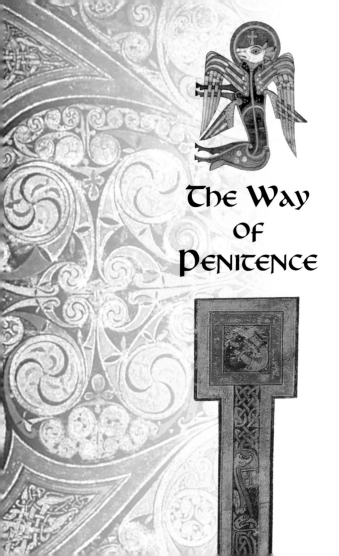

The Way
Of
Penitence

TRUTH WITHIN

When is a person able to testify to the souls of others? When he can testify to his own soul first. When is he capable of correcting others? When he can correct himself first.

The Alphabet of Devotion

THE DAY OF THE LORD

The day of the Lord, most righteous King of
    Kings, is at hand:
a day of anger and vindication, of darkness
    and of cloud,
a day of wonderful mighty thunders,
a day also of distress, of sorrow and sadness,
in which the love and desire of women will cease
and the striving of men and the desire of this
    world.

Columba, from the Altus Prosator

THE STRUGGLE

Shame on my thoughts, how they stray from me! I fear great danger from this on the Day of Eternal Judgement.

During the psalms they wander on a path that is not right; they run, they distract, they misbehave before the eyes of the great God...

One moment they follow ways of loveliness, and the next ways of riotous shame – no lie!...

O beloved truly chaste Christ, to whom every eye is clear, may the grace of the sevenfold Spirit come to keep them, to hold them in check!

Rule this heart of mine, O swift God of the elements, that you may be my love, and that I may do your will!

From the Leabhar Breac

By the Grace of God

By the grace of God Colum rose to exalted
    companionship
awaiting bright signs, he kept watch while he lived...
He was learning's pillar in every stronghold...
A sound, austere sage of Christ:
no fog of drink nor fog of delights —
he avoided the fill of his mouth.
He was holy, he was chaste,
he was charitable, a famous stone in victory.
He was a full light.
He was an ample fort for the stranger...
He was a shelter to the naked,
he was a teat to the poor...
His body's desire, he destroyed it...
He destroyed the darkness of envy,
he destroyed the darkness of jealousy...
He fought a long and noble battle against the flesh.

He was constant to the memory of the cross.
What he conceived keeping vigil,
by action he ascertained.

Extracts from The Amra Choluimb Chille

A Way Through the Storms

O helper of workers,
ruler of all the good,
guard on the ramparts
and defender of the faithful,
who lifts up the lowly
and crushes the proud,
ruler of the faithful,
enemy of the impenitent,
judge of all judges,
who punishes those who err,
pure life of the living,
light and Father of lights
shining with great light,
denying to none of the hopeful
your strength and help,
I beg that me, a little man
trembling and most wretched
rowing through the infinite storm of this age,
Christ may draw after Him to the lofty
most beautiful haven of life.

Columba, from the Adiutor Laborantium

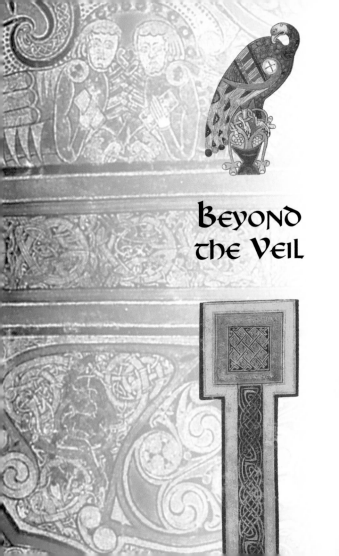

BEYOND
the VEIL

CROWDS OF ANGELS

The maker of all things,
The Lord God worship we:
Heaven white with angel's wings,
Earth and the white-waved sea.

Medieval Irish Poem

Were all the tribute of Scotia mine
From its midland to its borders,
I would give all for one little cell
In my beautiful Derry.
For its peace and for its purity,
For the white angels that go
In crowds from one end to the other.
I love my beautiful Derry
For its quietness and its purity,
For heaven's angels that come and go
Under every leaf of the oaks…

Attributed to St Columba

THE SPIRITUAL REALM

The High Creator, the Unbegotten Ancient of Days,
was without origin of beginning, limitless.
He is and He will be for endless ages of ages,
with whom is the only-begotten Christ,
    and the Holy Spirit,
co-eternal in the everlasting glory of divinity.
We do not confess three gods, but say one God,
saving our faith in three most glorious Persons.

He created good angels and archangels, the orders
of Principalities and Thrones, of Powers
    and of Virtues,
so that the goodness and majesty of the Trinity
might not be unproductive in all works of bounty,
but might have heavenly beings in which
    He might greatly
show forth his favours by a word of power.

Columba, from the Altus Prosator

HEALING POWER

On a certain day… the saint arose from reading, and said with a smile, 'I must now hasten to the oratory to pray to the Lord on behalf of a poor woman in Hibernia, who at this moment is suffering the pangs of a most difficult childbirth, and is calling upon the name of Columba. She trusteth that God will grant her relief from her sufferings through my prayers…'

Having said this, the saint, being touched with pity for the poor woman, hastened to the church, and, on his bended knees, earnestly prayed for her to Christ, who was Himself by birth a partaker of humanity. Returning from the church after his prayer, he said to the brethren who met him, 'The Lord Jesus, born of a woman, hath given seasonable help to this poor woman, and hath mercifully relieved her from her distress. She hath been safely delivered of a child, nor shall she die upon this occasion.'

Adamnan's Life of St Columba

THE CALL TO PRAYER

Another day, while Columba was in the mother
church [Iona], he suddenly smiled and called out:
'Colmán mac Beognai has set sail to come here,
and is now in great danger in the surging tides of
the whirlpool of Corryveckan. Sitting in the prow,
he lifts up his hands to heaven and blesses the
turbulent, terrible sea. Yet the Lord terrifies him
in this way, not so that the ship in which he sits
should be overwhelmed and wrecked by the waves,
but rather to rouse him to pray more fervently that
he may sail through the peril and reach us here.'

Adamnan's Life of Columba

THE HOUR OF DEPARTURE

As the happy hour of his departure gradually approached, the saint became silent. Then as soon as the bell tolled at midnight, he rose hastily, and went to the church; and running more quickly than the rest, he entered it alone, and knelt down in prayer beside the altar. At the same moment his attendant Diormit, who more slowly followed him, saw from a distance that the whole interior of the church was filled with a heavenly light in the direction of the saint. And as he drew near to the door, the same light he had seen, and which was also seen by a few more of the brethren standing at a distance, quickly disappeared. Diormit therefore entering the church, cried out in a mournful voice, 'Where art thou, father?' And feeling his way in the darkness, as the brethren had not yet brought in the lights, he found the saint lying before the altar; and raising him up a little, he sat down beside him, and laid his holy head on his bosom. Meanwhile the rest of the monks ran in hastily… with their lights, and beholding their dying father, burst into lamentations. And the saint, as we have been told by some who were present, even before his soul departed, opened wide his eyes and looked round him from side to side, with a countenance full of wonderful joy and gladness…

Diormit then raised the holy right hand of the saint, that he might bless his assembled monks. And the venerable father himself moved his hand at the same time, as well as he was able… And having given them his holy benediction in this way, he immediately breathed his last. After his soul had left the tabernacle of the body, his face still continued ruddy, and brightened in a wonderful way by his vision of the angels, and that to such a degree that he had the appearance, not so much of one dead, as of one alive and sleeping.

Adamnan's Life of St Columba

The Court
of Heaven

THE GUARDIAN ANGEL

Thou angel of God who hast charge of me
From the dear Father of mercifulness,
The shepherding kind of the fold of the saints
To make round about me this night;

Drive from me every temptation and danger,
Surround me on the sea of unrighteousness,
And in the narrows, crooks, and straits,
Keep thou my coracle, keep it always.

Be thou a bright flame before me,
Be thou a guiding star above me,
Be thou a smooth path below me,
And be a kindly shepherd behind me,
To-day, to-night, and for ever.

I am tired and I a stranger,
Lead thou me to the land of angels;
For me it is time to go home
To the court of Christ, to the peace of Heaven.

Carmina Gadelica

PEACE

O God, grant us thy peace,
the peace of men also,
the peace of St Columba, the kind,
and of St Mary mild, the loving one,
and of Christ, the king of human heart.

Traditional Gaelic

A Note on Sources

This collection of writings, from very diverse sources, has the shape of a pilgrimage about it. It is meant to be a journey, not into the past, but into the future illuminated by a long shaft of light from the sixth century. Few of these pieces can be definitely attributed to Columba, although many may bear his influence. The works that are generally agreed to be by him are in Latin, and of these the *Altus Prosator* is not so much a nature poem, of which there are so many in the celtic tradition, as a poem about the nature of God and about his sovereignty and judgment. The *Adiutor Laborantium* has a similar note of seriousness, and yet a touching – almost humorous note – of humility and frailty. This is, in all likelihood, the signature of Columba himself. The great eulogy, the *Amra Choluimb Chille* was composed by the poet Dallan Forgaill, probably in the court of the Irish King Aedh, on the death of Columba. Columcille, the warrior-prince who became a pilgrim, was celebrated above all for abandoning earthly warfare in favour of the spiritual battle, and this earliest testimony leaves us in no doubt about his uncompromising lifestyle. The *Alphabet of Devotion*, written by Colman mac Beognae, a pupil of Columba and founder of the monastery of Lann Elo, gives us the flavour of his master's simple and practical wisdom. The poet *Beccán mac Luigdech*, a poet and hermit from Iona in the mid-seventh century, celebrates his founder's questing spirit. However, the greatest source of all for Columba's life – a unique legacy from its time – is the biography by *Adamnan*, ninth abbot of Iona, written about 100 years after Columba's death. A few extracts can give the reader a sense of Adamnan's intimate and touching portrait which emerges strongly, even from miraculous and sometimes legendary material. It is easy to see why this man, once destined to be a king, was so loved by ordinary men and women. The truth is, Columba came to consider himself as ordinary, a humble servant, as is so eloquently described in the tenth century biography, *The Irish Life of Columcille*. A poem like the *Song of Trust*, another much later work, enshrines the legacy of his struggle against paganism. Columba may even have been tempted, in his early life, to misuse his spiritual gifts in a society which was still torn between druidic divination and the Christian gospel: a world, not unlike our own, that was easily impressed by magic and psychic phenomena, but also longed to find the lasting wisdom and security which Columba found ultimately in Christ himself. The *Rule of Columba* was also set down after his time, but it expresses a deep heritage of spirituality on Iona, a warmth of love combined with a rigorous determination to follow Christ. There is a profound yearning and a beauty in some of the works of later centuries which capture Columba's longing for the world he had relinquished and yet the glorious quest he had undertaken to contemplate the 'King of Heaven'. These works of medieval Irish poetry convey the grieving and the struggling penitent, as well as the lyrical celebration of the natural world in all its glory, which is so characteristic of the Columban spirit – steeped as the monks of Iona were in the poetry of the psalms, as well as in the splendour of their island world. Finally the great compendium of Gaelic songs and prayers, the *Carmina Gadelica*, gathered by Alexander Carmichael at the end of the last century, demonstrates so eloquently how the name and the spiritual influence of Columba have survived in Highland culture until the modern era. As regards the twentieth century, our own time has seen the remarkable birth of a new community on Iona and a growing, worldwide interest in the spirituality of the celtic Christian tradition. The God of Columba is the God of past, present and future history.

48